Remote Work Revolution:

A Guide to Finding the Perfect Remote Job

By Wanda James

Dedication

To all those individuals that are looking for their
next chapter, I hope this bring insight in your
journey.....

Content Blueprint

## Chapter 1: The Rise of Remote Work

- Introduction to the concept of remote work and its increasing popularity in the modern workforce.

- Discussion on the benefits and challenges of remote work arrangements.

## Chapter 2: Assessing Your Skills and Preferences

- Identifying your key skills, strengths, and areas of expertise that are relevant to remote job opportunities.

- Assessing your preferred working style, communication preferences, and work environment for remote work.

Chapter 3: Exploring Remote Job Opportunities

- Overview of different types of remote job positions available in various industries.

- Tips for researching and identifying remote job opportunities that match your skill set and interests.

Chapter 4: Building Your Remote Work Toolkit

- Overview of essential tools and technology for remote work, including communication platforms, project management tools, and time tracking software.

- Tips for setting up a productive home office space for remote work.

Chapter 5: Crafting a Standout Remote Job Application

- Guidelines for preparing a compelling resume and cover letter tailored to remote job positions.

- Tips for showcasing your remote work skills and experience during the application process.


Chapter 6: Navigating Remote Job Interviews

- Strategies for preparing for remote job interviews, including technical considerations and best practices for virtual interviews.

- Tips for effectively communicating your qualifications and expertise in a remote setting.

## Chapter 7: Negotiating Remote Work Arrangements

- Advice for negotiating your salary, benefits, working hours, and other terms of your remote job offer.

- Tips for setting boundaries and managing expectations in a remote work environment.

## Chapter 8: Establishing a Successful Remote Work Routine

- Guidance on creating a daily routine and work schedule that promotes productivity and work-life balance in a remote setting.

- Tips for staying motivated, focused, and connected while working remotely.

Chapter 9: Overcoming Remote Work Challenges

- Strategies for addressing common challenges of remote work, such as isolation, communication barriers, and time management issues.

- Tips for maintaining work-life balance and mental well-being in a remote work environment.


Chapter 10: Thriving in Your Remote Career

- Advice for continuous learning and professional development to enhance your remote work skills and advance your career.

- Tips for networking, building relationships, and growing your reputation as a successful remote worker.

Conclusion: Embracing the Future of Remote Work

- Final thoughts on the future trends and opportunities in remote work.

- Encouragement to embrace the flexibility, autonomy, and benefits of remote work for a fulfilling and rewarding career.


Bonus: Remote Working Terminology

This outline provides a structured approach to exploring, preparing for, and thriving in the remote work landscape, offering comprehensive guidance for individuals seeking to find the perfect remote job.

There are various remote job opportunities available for individuals seeking part-time work. Some popular part-time remote job options include:

1. **Virtual Assistant**: Virtual assistants provide administrative support to businesses or entrepreneurs from a remote location. Tasks may include email management, scheduling appointments, data entry, and more.

2. **Freelance Writer**: Freelance writers can support businesses by creating content such as articles, blog posts, social media posts, and more. This job offers flexibility in terms of working hours and projects.

3. **Online Tutor**: Online tutoring allows individuals to teach or mentor students in various subjects remotely. This job is ideal for those with expertise in specific academic areas.

4. **Customer Service Representative**: Many roles are available for remote customer service representatives who handle customer inquiries, provide support, and resolve issues via phone, chat, or email.

5. **Social Media Manager**: Social media managers help businesses manage their online presence by creating content, engaging with followers, and analyzing performance metrics.

6. **Graphic Designer**: Graphic designers create visual content for online and print media. They work on in creating logos, website graphics, marketing materials, and more.

7. **Virtual Bookkeeper**: Virtual bookkeepers assist businesses with maintaining financial records, processing invoices, and reconciling accounts remotely.

8. **Data Entry Specialist**: Data entry specialists input and manage data for businesses, organizations, or research projects from a remote location.

9. **Online Researcher**: Online researchers gather and organize data for businesses, academic institutions, or individuals using online resources.

10. **Online Moderator**: Online moderators monitor online communities, forums, or social media platforms to ensure they are safe and engaging for users.

These are just a few examples of part-time remote job opportunities available. Individuals can explore various job platforms, freelancing websites, and remote job boards to find part-time remote jobs that suit their skills and interests.

Here's a questionnaire to help you identify the right remote job for you:

1. What is your current professional background and experience?

2. What are your top skills or areas of expertise that you believe can be utilized in a remote job?

3. What type of remote work arrangement are you seeking (e.g., part-time, full-time, freelance, contract)?

4. What are your preferred or required working hours and schedule for a remote job?

5. Are there specific industries or sectors that interest you for remote work?

6. What remote job positions or roles align with your career goals and aspirations?

7. Do you have any certifications, qualifications, or credentials that would be relevant for remote job opportunities?

8. What remote work tools or software are you familiar with and proficient in using?

9. Are you comfortable with remote communication and collaboration tools (e.g., Slack, Zoom, and Microsoft Teams)?

10. What are your salary expectations or requirements for a remote job?

11. Are you open to flexible or project-based remote job opportunities?

12. Do you prefer working independently or as part of a remote team?

13. Have you researched remote job platforms or websites that specialize in offering remote job opportunities?

14. Are you willing to undergo training or acquire new skills to qualify for remote job positions that interest you?

15. How important is work-life balance and flexibility in a remote job for you?

By answering these questions, you can gain more clarity on what type of remote job would be the best fit for your skills, preferences, and career goals. This will help guide your search for the right remote job opportunity that aligns with your needs and aspirations.

Chapter 1: The Rise of Remote Work

Remote work, also known as telecommuting or telework, refers to the practice of working outside a traditional office setting, often from home or other locations. In recent years, remote work has seen a significant rise in popularity within the modern workforce. This shift has been driven by advancements in technology, changing attitudes towards work-life balance, and the increasing need for flexibility in employment arrangements.

One of the key benefits of remote work is the flexibility it offers to employees. Remote workers have the freedom to set their own schedules, work from anywhere with an internet connection, and avoid long commutes to a physical office. This flexibility can lead to greater job satisfaction, improved work-life balance, and increased productivity for individuals who thrive in autonomous work environments.

Another advantage of remote work is the potential cost savings for both employees and employers. Remote workers can save money on transportation, clothing, and meals typically associated with commuting to a physical office. Employers, in turn, can reduce overhead costs related to office space, utilities, and other expenses associated with maintaining a traditional workplace.

Despite the numerous benefits of remote work, there are also challenges that come with working outside a traditional office environment. One of the primary challenges is the potential for isolation and feelings of disconnection from coworkers and company culture. Remote workers may miss out on spontaneous interactions, team collaboration, and networking opportunities that are more readily available in a physical office setting.

Communication can also be a challenge in remote work arrangements. Without face-to-face interactions, remote workers must rely on virtual communication tools such as email, video conferencing, and messaging platforms to stay connected with colleagues. Miscommunications and misunderstandings can occur more easily in remote settings, requiring clear communication strategies and regular check-ins to ensure alignment and collaboration among team members.

Another challenge of remote work is the blurred boundaries between work and personal life. Without a physical separation between work and home, remote workers may struggle to disconnect from work responsibilities, leading to burnout and decreased work-life balance. Establishing boundaries, setting clear expectations, and maintaining a healthy routine are essential for maintaining well-being and productivity in a remote work environment.

Overall, the rise of remote work signifies a fundamental shift in how work is perceived and structured in the modern workforce. As more companies embrace remote work options and individuals seek greater flexibility in their careers, the benefits and challenges of remote work arrangements will continue to evolve. Understanding the factors driving the rise of remote work and navigating the opportunities and obstacles it presents are key to thriving in this evolving work landscape.

## Chapter 2: Assessing Your Skills and Preferences

Before embarking on a journey to find the perfect remote job, it's important to take stock of your skills, strengths, and preferences to align them with remote work opportunities. Begin by identifying your key skills and expertise that are relevant to remote job positions. Consider the tasks, projects, and responsibilities you excel at and how they can be translated into remote work settings. This self-assessment will help you narrow down potential job opportunities that align with your strengths.

In addition to evaluating your skills, it's essential to assess your preferred working style and communication preferences for remote work. Consider whether you thrive in a highly collaborative environment or if you prefer working independently. Reflect on how you communicate with colleagues, handle feedback, and seek support in virtual settings. Understanding your work preferences and communication style will guide you in selecting remote job opportunities that align with your desired work environment.

Remote work requires a level of self-discipline, motivation, and independence to succeed. Evaluate your ability to stay focused, manage time effectively, and meet deadlines without constant supervision. Assess your comfort level with using technology and remote work tools, such as video conferencing, project management software, and communication platforms. Developing these skills and traits will demonstrate your readiness for a remote work arrangement and enhance your chances of finding the right remote job.

As you assess your skills and preferences for remote work, consider your personal priorities and lifestyle preferences. Think about how remote work can better accommodate your individual needs, whether it's flexibility in scheduling, reduced commute time, or better work-life balance. By aligning your skills, preferences, and lifestyle goals with remote work opportunities, you can create a more fulfilling and sustainable career path that meets your professional and personal aspirations.

Reflect on your past experiences with remote work or telecommuting, if applicable. Identify what aspects of remote work you enjoyed or found challenging in previous roles. Use these insights to refine your remote work preferences, expectations, and boundaries moving forward. Learning from past experiences can help you navigate the remote work landscape more effectively and make informed decisions about potential job opportunities.

In summary, assessing your skills and preferences is a critical step in finding the right remote job that aligns with your strengths, work style, and personal goals. By conducting a thorough self-assessment, you can better understand your readiness for remote work, articulate your value to potential employers, and narrow down job opportunities that match your profile. Taking the time to evaluate your skills and preferences will set you on the path to a successful and fulfilling remote career.

Chapter 3: Exploring Remote Job Opportunities

In today's competitive job market, the ability to work remotely has become an increasingly popular and sought-after option for many individuals. There are a wide range of remote job opportunities available across various industries, allowing individuals to work from the comfort of their own home or from any location with an internet connection.

One of the key benefits of remote work is the flexibility it offers. Remote jobs often allow individuals to set their own hours and work at times that are convenient for them. This can be particularly appealing for individuals with families or other commitments that may make traditional office hours difficult.

Additionally, remote work can offer a better work-life balance, as there is often less time wasted commuting to and from the office. This can lead to increased productivity and job satisfaction, as individuals are able to focus on their work without the stress of a long commute.

Remote job opportunities can also provide a greater sense of freedom and independence. Working remotely allows individuals to create their own workspace that is comfortable and conducive to their productivity. This can lead to a more positive work environment and increased job satisfaction.

When it comes to finding remote job opportunities, there are a number of resources available to help individuals explore their options. Online job boards and freelance platforms are a great place to start, as they offer a wide range of remote job opportunities across various industries. Networking with other professionals in the field can also be a valuable tool for uncovering potential remote job opportunities.

It is important to research potential remote job opportunities thoroughly before applying, to ensure that the job aligns with your skills, experience, and career goals. Additionally, it is important to be prepared for a potential interview process, as many remote jobs may still require some level of virtual interaction with employers. With a little bit of preparation and research, individuals can uncover a wide range of remote job opportunities that can offer flexibility, independence, and a better work-life balance.

List of websites to seek remote work:

1. FlexJobs (www.flexjobs.com)

2. Remote.co (www.remote.co)

3. We Work Remotely (www.weworkremotely.com)

4. Remote OK (www.remoteok.io)

5. JustRemote (www.justremote.co)

6. Remotive (www.remotive.io)

7. Virtual Vocations (www.virtualvocations.com)

List of websites of overseas companies who hire remotely:

1. Buffer (www.buffer.com) - Buffer is a social media management company that hires remote workers from around the world.

2. Automattic (www.automattic.com) - The company behind WordPress, Automattic hires remote employees for various roles.

3. GitLab (about.gitlab.com) - GitLab is a software development company that operates entirely remotely, with team members located in over 65 countries.

4. Zapier (zapier.com) - Zapier is a workflow automation tool that hires remote employees to fill various positions.

5. Toptal (www.toptal.com) - Toptal is a network of top freelance software developers and designers, with a remote team working from different countries.

6. InVision (www.invisionapp.com) - InVision is a digital product design platform that hires remote employees for various positions.

7. Appen (www.appen.com) - Appen provides high-quality data for machine learning and AI applications and hires remote workers globally.

Chapter 4: Building Your Remote Work Toolkit

In the modern world of remote work, having the right tools and resources at your disposal is crucial for success. In this chapter, we will explore the essential components of a remote work toolkit and how you can leverage them to maximize your productivity and efficiency while working remotely.

1. Communication Tools: Effective communication is key in remote work settings. Utilize tools like Slack, Microsoft Teams, or Zoom to stay connected with your team members and collaborate on projects seamlessly. Set up regular check-ins and video calls to ensure everyone is on the same page and foster a sense of camaraderie within the team.

2. Project Management Software: Keeping track of tasks, deadlines, and progress is essential for

remote work success. Consider using project management tools like Asana, Trello, or Basecamp to organize your workflows, assign tasks, and monitor project milestones. These tools can help you stay organized and ensure that projects are completed on time.

3. Time Tracking and Productivity Tools: Working remotely requires a high level of self-discipline and time management. Use tools like Toggl, RescueTime, or Focus@Will to track your time, set goals, and eliminate distractions. These tools can help you stay focused, prioritize tasks, and increase your productivity while working from home.

4. Cloud Storage and File Sharing: Accessing and sharing files with team members is essential for remote collaboration. Use cloud storage services like Google Drive, Dropbox, or Microsoft OneDrive to store and share documents, presentations, and spreadsheets securely. These

tools make it easy to collaborate on projects and ensure that everyone has access to the latest versions of files.

5. Virtual Private Network (VPN): Protecting your online privacy and data security is crucial when working remotely. Use a VPN service like NordVPN, ExpressVPN, or CyberGhost to encrypt your internet connection and browse the web securely. A VPN can help you safely access company networks, protect sensitive information, and prevent cyber threats while working from different locations.

6. Online Collaboration Tools: Collaborating with team members in real-time is essential for remote work success. Consider using tools like Google Workspace, Microsoft Office 365, or Slack Connect to collaborate on documents, spreadsheets, and presentations. These tools facilitate seamless communication and

teamwork, making it easier to work together regardless of physical distance.

7. Ergonomic Equipment: Setting up a comfortable and ergonomic workspace is vital for remote work wellbeing. Invest in a good quality desk, chair, and monitor to create a conducive work environment. Consider using tools like standing desks, ergonomic keyboards, and mousepads to prevent strain and promote good posture while working remotely. Your physical workspace plays a significant role in your productivity and overall well-being while working from home.

8. Cybersecurity Tools: As remote work involves accessing company data and sensitive information from different locations, it is crucial to prioritize cybersecurity. Consider using antivirus software, firewall protection, and password management tools to safeguard your digital assets. Tools like LastPass, Bitdefender, and Norton Security can help protect your

devices and data from online threats, ensuring a secure remote work environment.

9. Virtual Meeting Platforms: With remote work becoming the new normal, virtual meetings have become a common occurrence. Utilize platforms like Zoom, Microsoft Teams, or Google Meet to conduct virtual meetings, webinars, and conference calls with team members and clients. These tools offer features like screen sharing, video conferencing, and chat options, making remote collaboration and communication more efficient and effective.

10. Wellness and Well-being Apps: Working remotely can blur the lines between work and personal life, leading to burnout and stress. To prioritize your well-being, consider using wellness apps like Headspace, Calm, or YogaGlo to practice mindfulness, meditation, and relaxation techniques. These apps can help you manage stress, improve focus, and maintain a

healthy work-life balance while working remotely, ensuring that you stay mentally and physically healthy. Prioritizing your well-being is essential for long-term success and fulfillment in a remote work environment.

In conclusion, building a comprehensive remote work toolkit is essential for maximizing your productivity, collaboration, and well-being in a remote work environment. By utilizing the right communication tools, project management software, time tracking resources, cloud storage services, VPNs, online collaboration tools, and ergonomic equipment, you can create a productive and efficient remote workspace. Experiment with different tools and find the ones that work best for your workflow and preferences to optimize your remote work experience.

Chapter 5: Crafting a Standout Remote Job Application

In the competitive world of remote work, it is essential to craft a standout job application to increase your chances of landing your desired remote job. In this chapter, we will explore key strategies and tips for creating a compelling remote job application that showcases your skills, experience, and suitability for remote work positions.

1. Customize Your Resume and Cover Letter: Tailor your resume and cover letter to highlight relevant skills, experiences, and accomplishments that align with the remote job requirements. Showcase your ability to work independently, communicate effectively, and manage time efficiently – qualities that are highly valued in remote work settings. Personalize your application to demonstrate your genuine interest in the role and company,

making a strong first impression on potential employers.

2. Highlight Remote Work Experience: If you have previous experience working remotely or in a virtual environment, make sure to emphasize it in your job application. Describe how you effectively managed projects, communicated with team members, and achieved results while working remotely. Highlight your ability to stay productive, motivated, and engaged in a remote work setting, showcasing your readiness for remote job opportunities.

3. Showcase Your Technical Skills: Remote work often requires proficiency in various digital tools and software. Highlight your technical skills, such as proficiency in project management tools, video conferencing platforms, and communication apps, in your job application. Demonstrate your ability to adapt to new technologies, troubleshoot issues

independently, and collaborate effectively in virtual environments, showcasing your readiness for remote work positions.

4. Provide Concrete Examples and Results: Back up your qualifications with concrete examples and results from your previous work experiences. Include measurable achievements, such as meeting project deadlines, increasing productivity, or improving processes, to demonstrate your impact and contributions in previous roles. Providing specific examples will help potential employers understand your capabilities and suitability for remote work positions.

5. Demonstrate Excellent Communication Skills: Clear and effective communication is crucial in remote work settings. Showcase your strong written and verbal communication skills in your job application by using professional language, addressing potential questions or concerns, and

demonstrating your ability to convey information clearly and concisely. Highlight your experience in collaborating with remote team members and clients to showcase your communication capabilities in virtual work environments.

6. Showcase Your Problem-Solving Skills: Remote work requires individuals to be self-sufficient and proactive in addressing challenges that may arise. Highlight your problem-solving skills in your job application by showcasing your ability to identify issues, propose solutions, and implement strategies to overcome obstacles. Demonstrate your resilience, adaptability, and creative thinking in previous work experiences to showcase your ability to navigate remote work challenges effectively.

7. Emphasize Your Time Management Abilities: Effective time management is essential for success in remote work environments where

individuals are responsible for managing their own schedules and priorities. Emphasize your time management skills in your job application by highlighting your ability to prioritize tasks, meet deadlines, and maintain a strong work ethic in virtual settings. Showcase your organization, planning, and multitasking abilities to demonstrate your readiness for remote work positions.

8. Show Your Passion for Remote Work: Convey your enthusiasm and passion for remote work in your job application to demonstrate your commitment and dedication to pursuing a career in virtual environments. Share your reasons for seeking remote work opportunities, how remote work aligns with your career goals and values, and your eagerness to contribute to a remote team. Showing your genuine interest in remote work will set you apart from other applicants and showcase your enthusiasm for the role and company. Crafting a standout remote job application requires careful attention to detail,

personalized customization, and strategic highlighting of your skills and experiences. By following these tips and strategies, you can create a compelling job application that resonates with potential employers and increases your chances of securing remote job opportunities.

Chapter 6: Navigating Remote Job Interviews

Remote job interviews have become increasingly common in today's digital age, requiring job seekers to adapt and prepare for virtual interactions with potential employers. In this chapter, we will explore essential tips and strategies for navigating remote job interviews effectively and making a strong impression in virtual settings.

1. Test Your Technology: Before the remote job interview, ensure that your technology is working smoothly. Test your internet connection, audio quality, and video settings to avoid any technical issues during the interview. Familiarize yourself with the video conferencing platform being used and ensure that you have a quiet and well-lit space for the interview to project professionalism and attentiveness.

2. Dress Professionally: Just like an in-person interview, it is important to dress professionally for a remote job interview. Choose appropriate attire that reflects the company's culture and industry, projecting a polished and presentable image. Dressing professionally can boost your confidence and create a positive first impression with potential employers, showcasing your respect for the interview process.

3. Prepare Your Environment: Create a professional and distraction-free environment for the remote job interview. Choose a quiet location with minimal background noise, clutter, or distractions to ensure that you can focus on the interview questions and engage effectively with the interviewer. Set up a clean and organized workspace that conveys professionalism and readiness for the interview.

4. Practice Active Listening: Actively listening and engaging with the interviewer is essential for a

successful remote job interview. Practice attentive listening by maintaining eye contact, nodding in agreement, and responding thoughtfully to questions. Avoid interruptions or distractions and demonstrate your interest in the conversation by asking relevant questions and providing thoughtful responses.

5. Research the Company: Prior to the remote job interview, conduct thorough research on the company, its values, culture, and recent achievements. Familiarize yourself with the company's products or services, industry trends, and key personnel to demonstrate your genuine interest in the role and company. Incorporate your knowledge of the company into your responses during the interview to showcase your preparedness and enthusiasm.

6. Highlight Your Remote Work Experience: If you have previous experience working remotely or in virtual settings, make sure to highlight it

during the interview. Share examples of how you effectively managed projects, communicated with colleagues, and achieved results while working remotely. Showcase your ability to adapt to virtual environments and stay productive and engaged in remote work settings to demonstrate your readiness for the role.

7. Prepare for Common Interview Questions: Anticipate and prepare for common interview questions that may be asked during remote job interviews. Practice your responses to questions about your experience, skills, strengths and weaknesses, and your suitability for the role. Be prepared to provide specific examples and anecdotes from your work experiences to support your answers and showcase your qualifications for the position.

8. Showcase Your Communication Skills: Effective communication skills are crucial in remote work environments. During the remote

job interview, demonstrate strong verbal communication by speaking clearly, concisely, and confidently. Use professional language and tone, listen actively to the interviewer, and articulate your thoughts and ideas effectively. Showcase your ability to communicate professionally and clearly in virtual settings to impress potential employers.

9. Demonstrate Your Problem-Solving Abilities: Remote work often requires individuals to be independent problem-solvers. Showcase your problem-solving skills during the interview by discussing how you have identified and addressed challenges in previous work experiences. Share examples of how you have overcome obstacles, proposed innovative solutions, and demonstrated resilience and adaptability in navigating difficult situations. Highlighting your problem-solving abilities will show potential employers your readiness for remote work positions.

10. Follow-Up After the Interview: After the remote job interview, send a thank-you email to the interviewer to express your gratitude for the opportunity and reiterate your interest in the position. Use this opportunity to recap key points discussed during the interview, highlight your qualifications, and express your enthusiasm for the role. Reiterate your interest in the company and the value you can bring to the team to leave a positive impression with potential employers.

In conclusion, navigating remote job interviews requires careful preparation, attention to detail, and effective communication skills. By following these tips and strategies, you can make a strong impression during remote job interviews, showcase your qualifications and suitability for remote work positions, and increase your chances of securing your desired remote job opportunities. Remember to stay confident, professional, and engaged during remote job interviews to convey your readiness and enthusiasm for virtual work environments.

Chapter 7: Navigating Remote Job Arrangements

With the increasing popularity of remote work, it is essential for professionals to navigate remote job arrangements effectively to ensure productivity, work-life balance, and successful communication with colleagues and supervisors. In this chapter, we will explore key strategies and best practices for navigating remote job arrangements and maximizing efficiency and satisfaction in virtual work settings.

1. Establish a Structured Routine: Maintaining a structured routine is crucial for remote workers to stay organized and productive. Set a consistent schedule for your workday, including designated work hours, breaks, and tasks to complete. Create a daily or weekly schedule that outlines your priorities, deadlines, and goals to help you stay on track and manage your time effectively while working remotely.

2. Create a Dedicated Workspace: Designating a dedicated workspace for remote work can help create boundaries between work and personal life and boost productivity. Choose a quiet and well-equipped area in your home to serve as your home office, with a comfortable chair, desk, and necessary work supplies. Personalize your workspace with inspiring decor or plants to create a motivating and conducive environment for focused work.

3. Communicate Effectively with Colleagues: Effective communication is key to successful remote work arrangements. Stay connected with colleagues and supervisors through regular check-ins, team meetings, and collaboration tools such as email, instant messaging, or video conferencing. Maintain open and transparent communication with your team to share updates, progress, and challenges, and seek feedback or assistance when needed to foster a collaborative work environment.

4. Set Clear Goals and Expectations: Clarifying goals, expectations, and deliverables with supervisors or clients is essential for navigating remote job arrangements successfully. Establish clear objectives and timelines for your projects or tasks to ensure alignment with stakeholders and avoid misunderstandings. Regularly review and assess your progress towards meeting goals and adjust your strategies as needed to stay on track and achieve desired outcomes in remote work settings.

5. Practice Self-Care and Work-Life Balance: Maintaining a healthy work-life balance is crucial for remote workers to prevent burnout and maintain well-being. Prioritize self-care by taking breaks, staying active, and setting boundaries between work and personal life to avoid overworking. Practice mindfulness techniques, hobbies, or relaxation exercises to recharge and de-stress after work hours, promoting a healthy balance between work responsibilities and personal well-being in remote job arrangements.

In conclusion, navigating remote job arrangements requires establishing routines, communication, goal-setting, and self-care practices to promote productivity, well-being and success in virtual work environments. By following these strategies and best practices, remote workers can effectively manage their time, responsibilities, and relationships with colleagues, ensuring a positive and fulfilling remote work experience. Stay organized, communicative, and balanced to navigate remote job arrangements successfully and thrive in virtual work settings.

Chapter 8: Establishing a Successful Remote Work Routine

Establishing a successful remote work routine is essential for remote workers to maintain productivity, focus, and work-life balance in virtual work environments. In this chapter, we will delve into key strategies and tips for creating and maintaining a productive and structured remote work routine that fosters efficiency and well-being.

1. Set Clear Work Hours: Establishing clear work hours is crucial for remote workers to delineate between work time and personal time. Define your designated work hours based on your schedule, team collaboration needs, and personal preferences. Communicate your availability and work hours with colleagues and supervisors to set expectations and ensure effective communication and collaboration during remote work hours.

2. Create a Morning Routine: Starting your workday with a morning routine can help set a positive tone and prepare you for a productive day of remote work. Develop a routine that includes activities such as exercise, meditation, breakfast, and setting goals for the day. Incorporating a morning routine can boost your energy, focus, and motivation, setting the stage for a successful and focused remote workday.

3. Prioritize Tasks and Goals: Prioritizing tasks and goals is essential for remote workers to manage their workload effectively and stay on track with deadlines and deliverables. Create a daily or weekly to-do list that outlines your priorities, deadlines, and tasks to complete. Break down larger projects into smaller, manageable tasks to stay organized and focused on your goals, optimizing your productivity and progress in remote work settings.

4. Take Regular Breaks: Taking regular breaks throughout the workday is crucial for maintaining focus, energy, and well-being while working remotely. Incorporate short breaks between tasks or meetings to recharge, stretch, hydrate, or engage in mindfulness exercises. Schedule longer breaks for lunch or physical activity to rest and rejuvenate, promoting mental clarity, creativity, and overall well-being in remote work routines.

5. End the Workday with a Routine: Concluding your workday with a routine can help you mentally transition from work to personal time and establish boundaries to prevent overworking in remote settings. Create an end-of-day routine that includes reviewing your accomplishments, setting goals for the next day, and shutting down your workspace. Engage in activities such as exercise, relaxation, or hobbies to unwind and detach from work responsibilities, fostering a healthy work-life balance in remote work routines.

6. Stay Connected with Colleagues: Maintaining connections with colleagues is essential for remote workers to foster a sense of teamwork, collaboration, and camaraderie. Utilize communication tools such as video conferencing, instant messaging, or virtual team meetings to stay in touch with team members, share updates, and engage in collaborative projects. Build relationships with colleagues through informal chats, virtual coffee breaks, or team-building activities to strengthen connections and enhance teamwork in remote work routines.

7. Limit Distractions: Minimizing distractions is crucial for remote workers to maintain focus, productivity, and efficiency in virtual work environments. Identify potential distractions in your home workspace, such as noise, clutter, or personal tasks, and take steps to mitigate them. Establish boundaries with family members or housemates, set phone notifications, or use productivity tools to minimize distractions and

optimize your concentration and performance while working remotely.

8. Embrace Flexibility: Embracing flexibility is key for remote workers to adapt to changing priorities, schedules, and work dynamics in virtual work arrangements. Flexibility allows you to adjust your work hours, tasks, or environment to meet your needs and respond to unexpected challenges or opportunities. Find a balance between structure and flexibility in your remote work routine to accommodate personal responsibilities, preferences, and unforeseen circumstances, enabling you to maintain productivity and well-being in dynamic work settings.

9. Seek Professional Development Opportunities: Investing in professional development is essential for remote workers to enhance their skills, knowledge, and career growth in virtual work environments. Take

advantage of online courses, webinars, or virtual workshops to acquire new skills, certifications, or insights relevant to your field. Seek mentorship, coaching, or networking opportunities to expand your professional network, gain feedback, and advance your career prospects in remote work settings, demonstrating a commitment to continuous learning and growth as a remote professional.

10. Reflect and Adapt: Reflecting on your remote work routine and performance is crucial for identifying strengths, areas for improvement, and opportunities for growth in virtual work settings. Regularly assess your productivity, well-being, and satisfaction with your remote work arrangements to determine what is working well and what can be adjusted. Evaluate your goals, strategies, and outcomes to make informed decisions, adapt your routine, and optimize your remote work experience for continued success and fulfillment as a remote professional.

In summary, establishing a successful remote work routine involves setting clear work hours, creating morning and end-of-day routines, prioritizing tasks, taking breaks, and preserving work-life balance. By following these strategies and tips, remote workers can optimize their productivity, focus, and well-being in virtual work settings, ensuring a balanced and fulfilling remote work experience. Stay disciplined, organized, and mindful in establishing a successful remote work routine to enhance your effectiveness and satisfaction in remote work arrangements.

Chapter 9: Overcoming Remote Work Challenges

Remote work offers numerous benefits, such as flexibility, autonomy, and work-life balance. However, it also presents unique challenges that can impact productivity, communication, and well-being. In this chapter, we will explore common remote work challenges and provide strategies for overcoming them to thrive in virtual work environments.

1. Communication Barriers: One of the most significant challenges of remote work is communication barriers that can hinder collaboration, information sharing, and team cohesion. To overcome communication challenges, remote workers should prioritize clear and frequent communication with colleagues using various channels such as video calls, instant messaging, and email. Establish communication norms, guidelines, and expectations with team members to ensure

effective information sharing, feedback, and alignment in virtual work settings.

2. Feelings of Isolation: Working remotely can lead to feelings of isolation, disconnection, and loneliness due to physical separation from colleagues and limited opportunities for social interaction. To combat feelings of isolation, remote workers should intentionally nurture social connections, build relationships with colleagues, and engage in virtual team-building activities. Participate in virtual social events, coffee chats, or group discussions to connect with teammates, share experiences, and foster a sense of belonging and camaraderie in remote work environments.

3. Lack of Structure: Remote work can lack the structure and routine of traditional office settings, making it challenging for some remote workers to maintain focus, productivity, and work-life balance. To address the lack of

structure, establish a daily routine, set clear work hours, and create a designated workspace that mimics the structure and boundaries of a traditional office. Plan your tasks, breaks, and goals to stay organized and focused, optimizing your productivity and well-being in remote work routines.

4. Technology Issues: Technical difficulties and technology failures can disrupt workflow, communication, and collaboration in remote work environments, leading to frustration and delays in productivity. To tackle technology issues, ensure you have reliable internet connectivity, up-to-date software, and technical support resources to troubleshoot problems promptly. Learn how to use collaboration tools effectively, back up your data, and stay informed about cybersecurity best practices to mitigate technology-related challenges and maintain seamless remote work operations.

5. Work-Life Imbalance: Balancing work responsibilities with personal life can be a struggle for remote workers, as the lines between work and home can blur in virtual work arrangements. To overcome work-life imbalance, set boundaries between work and personal time, establish clear work hours, and prioritize self-care activities to recharge and rejuvenate. Schedule breaks, exercise routines, and social interactions to separate work tasks from personal commitments, fostering a healthy work-life balance and well-being in remote work routines.

6. Distractions and Procrastination: Remote work environments can be prone to distractions, such as household chores, family interruptions, or social media temptations, that can impede focus, concentration, and productivity. To combat distractions and procrastination, create a dedicated workspace, set boundaries with family members or housemates, and use productivity tools to stay on task. Practice time

management techniques, such as the Pomodoro method or time blocking, to structure your workday, prioritize tasks, and minimize distractions, enhancing your efficiency and motivation in remote work settings.

7. Career Development Opportunities: Remote work may pose challenges for career advancement, professional growth, and visibility within organizations, as remote workers may have limited access to networking, mentorship, and training opportunities compared to in-office employees. To overcome career development challenges, seek out virtual networking events, online learning platforms, and mentorship programs to expand your professional network, acquire new skills, and seek feedback from colleagues and supervisors. Advocate for career development opportunities, express your career goals, and demonstrate your skills and achievements to make valuable contributions and progress in your career as a remote professional.

Chapter 10: Thriving in Your Remote Work Career

Working remotely can offer numerous opportunities for personal growth, professional development, and career success when approached with intention, discipline, and adaptability. In this chapter, we will explore strategies for thriving in your remote work career and maximizing your potential in virtual work environments.

1. Establish Clear Goals: To thrive in your remote work career, it is essential to set clear goals, objectives, and milestones that align with your professional aspirations and organizational priorities. Define short-term and long-term goals, identify key performance indicators, and outline a roadmap for achieving success in your remote work career. Regularly review and adjust your goals based on feedback, changing circumstances, and personal growth to stay

focused and motivated in pursuing your career objectives.

2. Develop a Growth Mindset: Cultivating a growth mindset is crucial for thriving in your remote work career, as it enables you to embrace challenges, learn from failures, and continuously develop new skills and competencies. Embrace a positive attitude towards learning, experimentation, and feedback, viewing setbacks as opportunities for growth and improvement. Seek out challenges, take risks, and push yourself out of your comfort zone to expand your capabilities, enhance your resilience, and unlock your full potential as a remote professional.

3. Prioritize Self-Care: Prioritizing self-care is essential for maintaining physical, mental, and emotional well-being while navigating the demands and pressures of remote work. Make time for self-care activities, such as exercise,

mindfulness, hobbies, or social connections, to recharge, decompress, and stay energized throughout your remote work day. Establish boundaries between work and personal time, practice stress management techniques, and seek support from friends, family, or mental health professionals to address burnout, loneliness, or other challenges that may arise in remote work environments.

4. Cultivate Relationships: Building and nurturing relationships with colleagues, supervisors, mentors, and industry peers is crucial for thriving in your remote work career, as it enhances collaboration, feedback, and networking opportunities in virtual work settings. Reach out to colleagues for support, feedback, and mentorship, engage in virtual coffee chats, networking events, or professional communities to connect with like-minded professionals and expand your professional network. Foster trust, respect, and effective communication with team members to strengthen relationships, foster

teamwork, and enhance your career prospects as a remote professional.

5. Seek Feedback and Development Opportunities: Proactively seeking feedback, performance evaluations, and developmental opportunities is essential for growth, learning, and advancement in your remote work career. Request feedback from colleagues, supervisors, or mentors on your work performance, skills development, and career aspirations to gain insights, identify areas for improvement, and chart a path for professional growth. Participate in training programs, skills development workshops, or mentorship initiatives to acquire new skills, knowledge, and perspectives that can enhance your capabilities and elevate your career prospects in remote work environments.

6. Demonstrate Accountability and Results: Demonstrating accountability, reliability, and results-driven performance is crucial for

establishing credibility, trust, and impact as a remote professional. Take ownership of your work responsibilities, meet deadlines, and deliver high-quality results consistently to build a reputation for excellence and reliability in virtual work environments. Communicate proactively, seek clarification on tasks, and provide updates on your progress to keep stakeholders informed and demonstrate your commitment to achieving results and contributing value to your organization as a remote worker.

7. Embrace Continuous Learning: Embracing a mindset of continuous learning, growth, and adaptation is essential for thriving in your remote work career, as it enables you to stay relevant, agile, and resilient in evolving work landscapes. Stay curious, seek out new learning opportunities, and stay informed about industry trends, innovations, and best practices to expand your knowledge, skills, and capabilities as a remote professional. Engage in ongoing

professional development, pursue certifications, and attend virtual conferences, webinars, or workshops to stay ahead of the curve and position yourself for success in remote work careers.

8. Maintain Work-Life Balance: Striking a healthy balance between work responsibilities and personal well-being is crucial for thriving in your remote work career and sustaining long-term performance and satisfaction in virtual work settings. Set boundaries between work and personal time, establish a routine, and prioritize self-care activities to prevent burnout, maintain energy, and enhance your overall well-being as a remote professional. Schedule breaks, exercise, hobbies, or social interactions to recharge, refocus, and nurture your mental and emotional health while navigating the demands of remote work.

9. Foster Adaptability and Resilience: Cultivating adaptability, resilience, and agility is key for thriving in your remote work career, as it enables you to navigate uncertainty, challenges, and change with poise, creativity, and effectiveness. Embrace change as an opportunity for growth, remain flexible in response to unexpected circumstances, and adapt your strategies, goals, and routines to evolving work dynamics and priorities in remote work environments. Develop coping mechanisms, problem-solving skills, and stress management techniques to build resilience, bounce back from setbacks, and thrive in the face of adversity as a remote professional.

10. Celebrate Achievements and Milestones: Celebrating achievements, milestones, and successes is essential for maintaining motivation, morale, and a sense of accomplishment in your remote work career journey. Acknowledge and reward your progress, recognize your accomplishments, and

commemorate milestones, whether big or small, to cultivate a positive mindset, boost your confidence, and fuel your drive to excel in remote work environments. Share your successes, express gratitude to supporters, and reflect on your growth and achievements to stay motivated, inspired, and committed to pursuing excellence and thriving in your remote work career.

By implementing these strategies and approaches, you can position yourself for success, fulfillment, and growth in your remote work career, leveraging the opportunities and challenges of virtual work environments to thrive and reach your full potential as a remote professional.

As the world continues to embrace the future of remote work, it becomes increasingly evident that this work model is not merely a temporary response to external forces but a long-term trend that has the potential to revolutionize the way we work. With advancements in technology, communication tools, and remote collaboration platforms, the opportunities for individuals to work from anywhere in the world are expanding at a rapid pace. Embracing these future trends in remote work can lead to increased productivity, improved work-life balance, and enhanced job satisfaction.

In today's fast-paced and ever-evolving work environment, remote work offers a unique opportunity for individuals to take control of their schedules, workspaces, and overall professional experiences. The flexibility and autonomy that come with remote work enable employees to tailor their work routines to suit their preferences and personal needs, leading to a more balanced and fulfilling career. By embracing remote work, individuals can enjoy the benefits of a more flexible lifestyle, reduced commuting stress, and increased opportunities for personal growth and development.

Remote work presents a wealth of opportunities for individuals to connect with diverse teams and collaborate on projects with professionals from different backgrounds and locations. With the rise of virtual teams and remote collaboration tools, the boundaries of traditional office settings are being transcended, allowing for a more inclusive and global work environment. By embracing remote work, individuals can expand their networks, gain exposure to new ideas and perspectives, and enhance their skills through cross-cultural collaboration.

It is essential for professionals to recognize the potential of remote work as a valuable and sustainable career option in today's digital age.

By leveraging the opportunities and benefits that remote work offers, individuals can thrive in their careers, achieve work-life balance, and foster a sense of autonomy and empowerment in their professional lives. Embracing the future of remote work requires openness to change, adaptability to new ways of working, and a proactive mindset to capitalize on the endless possibilities that remote work has to offer.

In conclusion, as we navigate the complexities of the modern work landscape, it is crucial to embrace the future of remote work with enthusiasm, curiosity, and determination. By seizing the opportunities presented by remote work, individuals can redefine their career paths, enhance their professional experiences, and create a fulfilling and rewarding work-life balance. With the right mindset and a commitment to continuous learning and growth, remote work can be a transformative force in shaping the future of work and

unlocking new horizons of possibility for
individuals around the world.

Bonus: Remote Job Terminology to Know

1. Remote Work: Refers to a work arrangement in which employees work from a location outside of a traditional office setting, typically from home or a co-working space.

2. Telecommuting: Also known as telework, it involves working remotely and using telecommunication technology to perform job responsibilities.

3. Virtual Team: A group of individuals working together on projects and initiatives while geographically dispersed, relying on digital communication tools and collaboration platforms.

4. Work-from-Home (WFH): An abbreviation commonly used to refer to the practice of working remotely from one's residence.

5. Distributed Team: A team with members located in different geographic locations, working together on various projects and tasks.

6. Digital Nomad: A person who works remotely while traveling and changing locations frequently, often relying on technology to stay connected and productive.

7. Remote-first: An organizational approach where remote work is prioritized and integrated into the company culture and operations from the outset.

8. Asynchronous Communication: Communication that does not require real-time interaction, allowing employees to connect and collaborate without being online simultaneously.

9. Synchronous Communication: Real-time communication methods, such as video calls or instant messaging, where individuals interact simultaneously.

10. Remote Collaboration Tools: Software and platforms designed to facilitate communication, project management, and collaboration among remote teams, such as Zoom, Slack, and Trello.

11. Remote Work Policy: Guidelines and procedures established by organizations to govern remote work arrangements, including expectations, responsibilities, and communication protocols.

12. Flexibility: The ability to adjust work schedules, tasks, and locations to accommodate personal needs and preferences while working remotely.

13. Digital Workspace: A virtual environment where employees can access tools, resources, and information necessary for their remote work tasks.

14. Time Zone Difference: Variances in time zones between remote team members, requiring coordination and flexibility in scheduling meetings and activities.

15. Remote Onboarding: The process of integrating new employees into a remote work environment, providing them with the necessary training, resources, and support to succeed in their roles.

16. Remote Work Etiquette: Guidelines and best practices for effective communication, professionalism, and collaboration in remote work settings, including respecting boundaries,

setting clear expectations, and maintaining a positive attitude.

17. Remote Work/Life Integration: The concept of blending professional responsibilities with personal activities and priorities in a way that promotes work-life balance and overall well-being while working remotely.

18. Remote Work Security: Measures and protocols implemented to ensure the protection of sensitive data, information, and systems while employees work remotely, such as using secure networks, VPNs, and encryption tools.

19. Remote Work Benefits: Perks and advantages offered to employees who work remotely, including flexibility, autonomy, reduced commute times, increased productivity, and improved work-life balance.

20. Remote Work Challenges: Obstacles and issues that may arise in remote work environments, such as communication barriers, feelings of isolation, difficulties in team collaboration, and work-life integration struggles, requiring proactive solutions and strategies to overcome.

Best Wishes on your journey

www.ingramcontent.com/pod-product-compliance
Lightning Source LLC
La Vergne TN
LVHW051539050326
832903LV00033B/4340